CAROLE MARSH
MYSTERIES™

The Mystery on Alaska's
IDITAROD TRAIL

Teacher's Guide

by
Carole Marsh

Editors: Jenny Corsey, Sheila Phinazee & Teresa Valentine • Art & Design: Lynette Rowe

CAROLE MARSH BOOKS

GALLOPADE INTERNATIONAL

P.O. Box 2779 • Peachtree City, GA 30269
Tel: (800) 536-2438 • Fax: (800) 871-2979
email: orders@gallopade.com
www.gallopade.com

#1 THE MYSTERY OF BILTMORE HOUSE

#2 THE MYSTERY AT THE BOSTON MARATHON

#3 THE MYSTERY OF BLACKBEARD THE PIRATE

#4 THE MYSTERY OF THE ALAMO GHOST

#5 THE MYSTERY ON THE CALIFORNIA MISSION TRAIL

#6 THE MYSTERY OF THE CHICAGO DINOSAURS

#7 THE WHITE HOUSE CHRISTMAS MYSTERY

#8 THE MYSTERY ON ALASKA'S IDITAROD TRAIL

#9 THE MYSTERY AT KILL DEVIL HILLS

#10 THE MYSTERY IN NEW YORK CITY

#11 THE MYSTERY AT DISNEY WORLD

#12 THE MYSTERY ON THE UNDERGROUND RAILROAD

#13 THE MYSTERY IN THE ROCKY MOUNTAINS

#14 THE MYSTERY ON THE MIGHTY MISSISSIPPI

#15 THE MYSTERY AT THE KENTUCKY DERBY

#16 THE GHOST OF THE GRAND CANYON

©Carole Marsh • Gallopade International
800-536-2GET • www.gallopade.com

Dear Teachers,

In 1979, I began writing children's mysteries set at historic sites that still existed—primarily so that kids could go and see what they had read about. Frankly, I found no more fun, educational, and stress-free (actually, just plain joyful!) activity to do with my then school-age children than to visit a fascinating historic site!

People say that Alaska is one of the most beautiful places in America. Everyone should visit this place at least once! It's also one gigantic history lesson! At every site, I tried to introduce the who, what, when, where, why, and how. Not only has it been surprising to me how fascinated the kids are in real life, but it is amazing to also witness the depth of their interest. The first set of these magical experiences eventually transcended into a lifelong ongoing connection between me and my children.

We learned a lot, but what we learned best is that kids and adults can learn together. Reading and going and seeing and doing is what education is all about, and most especially, that "adopting" a subject or place leads to a lifelong interest in an era, a place, the people, and all the fascinating facts that made up their lives. We learned that history is still "living" and is not lost on kids! In fact, it is quite a revelation!

Enjoy your Alaska Iditarod Trail and studies,

Carole Marsh

4

Table of Contents

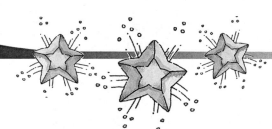

Page-by-Page Guide 7

Page-by-Page Guide 8

Page-by-Page Guide 9

Page-by-Page Guide 10

Page-by-Page Guide 11

Page-by-Page Guide 12

Page-by-Page Guide 13

Page-by-Page Guide 14

Page-by-Page Guide 15

Discussion Questions 16

Find It! 17

Calculate It! 18

Write It! 19

Spell It! 20

Create It! 21

Cook It! 22

Reproducible Iditarod Trail Maze 23

Reproducible Pair Up 24

Reproducible Dog Sled Craft 25

Reproducible Sourdough Expedition Rebus 26

Reproducible Word Search 27

Reproducible Fill-in-the-Blank Crossword 28

Reproducible Matching Characters 29

Reproducible Quiz 30

Reproducible True or False 31

Answer Key 32

Alaska Tourist Information

There are several ways to experience Alaska. Cruises, biking tours, fishing trips, train, bus, kayaking river trips, car, airplane, adventure tours, hiking tours, skiing tours, even by dog sled!

Alaska Division of Tourism
P.O. Box 110801
Juneau, Alaska 99811
Tel: (907) 465-2012
Fax: (907) 465-5442

Write to this department for a free copy of the Alaska Vacation Planner, which is packed full of Alaska facts and directories of where to stay, eat, and tour.

The Mystery on Alaska's
IDITAROD TRAIL

20 YEARS AGO . . .

As a mother and an author, one of the fondest periods of my life was when I decided to write mystery books for children. At this time (1979) kids were pretty much glued to the TV, something parents and teachers complained about the way they do about video games today.

I decided to set each mystery in a real place—a place kids could go and visit for themselves after reading the book. And I also used real children as characters. Usually a couple of my own children served as characters, and I had no trouble recruiting kids from the book's location to also be characters.

Also, I wanted all the kids—boys and girls of all ages—to participate in solving the mystery. And, I wanted kids to learn something as they read. Something about the history of the location. And I wanted the stories to be funny.

That formula of real+scary+smart+fun served me well. The kids and I had a great time visiting each site and many of the events in the stories actually came out of our experiences there. (For example, we really did pan for gold, mush twelve Huskies down a stretch of the Iditarod Trail, and eat Reindeer Stew!)

I love getting letters from teachers and parents who say they read the book with their class or child, then visited the historic site and saw all the places in the mystery for themselves. What's so great about that? What's great is that you and your children have an experience that bonds you together forever. Something you shared. Something you both cared about at the time. Something that crossed all age levels—a good story, a good scare, a good laugh!

20 years later,

Carole Marsh

Events and Activities

Iditarod Trail Sled Dog Race
www.iditarod.com
Anchorage, March

World Eskimo-Indian Olympics
Fairbanks, May

Savoonga Walrus Festival
St. Lawrence Island, May

Polar Bear Swim
Bering Sea, Nome, May

Moose Drooping Festival
Talkeetna, July

Fur Rendezvous (features 150 events including the World Championship Spring Sled Dog Race)
Anchorage, February

North Pole Winter Carnival
Homer, March

World Extreme Skiing Championship
Valdez, April

6

Page-by-page Guide

Alaska State Facts

Page #	Subject	EXPLORE!
1	Geography	What do you imagine when you think of Alaska?
1	Vocabulary	Alaska means the "Great Land." It is the biggest state in America.
2	Life	It's hard to wait, especially for something really good. What can you do to make waiting easier?
3	Sports	What sport is popular in your state?
4	Math	How many years has it been since the first woman won the Iditarod in 1985?
5	Geography	Mt. McKinley is the tallest peak in Alaska. It is also the tallest peak in North America. It is 20,320 feet above sea level. About 80 of Alaska's mountains are really volcanoes!
5	Vocabulary	A glacier is a huge mass of moving ice that originates from compacted snow. There are about 100,000 glaciers in Alaska.
6	Safety	Why is it important to wait for the pilot to turn on the signal before you unbuckle your seatbelt?
9	History	The first time gold was found in Alaska was in the southeast part of the state in 1880. The town formed from this gold rush is called Juneau.
9	Weather	Why do you think it gets so cold in Alaska? [The north gets colder than the south because it is farther away from the equator. How cold does it get? [In the winter, the temperature is about -30°F in the north or 20°F

State Capital: Juneau

State Flag: Gold stars, in the shape of the Big Dipper and the North Star, on a dark blue background. The gold color stands for the Alaskan Gold Rush, and the stars show the northern location of Alaska.

State Motto: "North to the future." The motto means that Alaska is a land of promise.

State Bird: Willow Ptarmigan (tar-mi-gan), a pheasant-like bird whose brown feathers turn snow white in the winter.

State Insect: Four-spot Skimmer Dragonfly, which lives around streams and ponds.

State Fish: King Salmon. Giant king salmon can weigh up to 100 pounds (45 kilograms)! Salmon are critical to Native Alaskan fishers and commercial fisherman.

State Land Mammal: Moose, the largest members of the deer family.

7

Alaska State Facts

(continued)

in the south. In the Alaskan summer, it is 39°F in the north or 60°F in the south.

9	Logic	Why does winter packing take more space? [Need more clothes, need thicker clothes, etc.]
10	Animal	Moles are small, insectivorous animals that burrow into the ground. They usually have poor eyesight and live under ground where it is dark.
12	Life	If you could have daylight for almost 24 hours, how would you spend your time?
14	Logic	Do you think Gold Dust Soup is real?
14	Geography	 Since we have 50 states all together, why do Alaskans call the other states the lower 48 instead of the lower 49? [Hawaii is not included because it is also a state that is not connected to other states.]
15	Health	Can you think of any other diseases that require vaccinations? [measles, mumps, rubella, etc.]
15	Geography	Alaska is only 50 miles from Russia, but it is more than 500 miles from the closest state.
16	Manners	Why do we tip? [Servers depend on the tip for their income because they earn a low "per hour" wage. 15% is a standard, more for great service.]
16	Culture	Seventy-five percent of Alaskans are Caucasian. Many have German, English, or Irish backgrounds. Sixteen percent are Native American, more than any other state. Other Alaskans are Hispanic, African American, Korean, or other Native American groups.

State Flower: Forget-Me-Not, a blue flower with a yellow center. They look frail but are actually hardy enough to survive cold Alaskan weather.

State Marine Mammal: Bowhead Whale. These beautiful creatures were nearly wiped out in the late 1880s by commercial whaling. According to today's laws, they may only be hunted by or for Native Alaskans!

State Tree: The Sitka Spruce (an evergreen tree) – the biggest and fastest-growing of all spruce trees.

State Gemstone: Jade, which comes in many different shades of green, brown, black, yellow, white, and red.

State Sport: You guessed it.... Sled Dog Racing! The Iditarod and the Quest International Sled Dog Race are two of the most famous races that take place.

THE LAST FRONTIER

8

Page-by-page Guide

Snow

A musher will find many different kinds of snow in Alaska. Here are some terms used to describe snow:

Snowpack: the depth of new and old snow together

Sugar snow: snow soft enough for animals to burrow through

Metamorphose: snow that is changing

Depth hoar: large, cup-shaped crystals

Firnification: the thawing and re-freezing of snow

Temperature gradient: snow that is growing in size

Spicules: snow with protrusions of ice

Needle ice: ice which forms in soil and can destroy plants

Permafrost: permanently frozen ground

Rime frost: wind-blown snow that can accumulate on trees or the fur of large animals

Lenses: frozen layers of ice that may keep animals from getting where they need to go

Ice layers: frozen ground that may prevent animals from grazing

Glacier fire: a type of highly reflective crusted ice

20	Weather	Have you ever played in snow? How would you play, if it were snowing right now? [sledding, snowball fight, etc.]

21   Animals   Other animals native to Alaska are bears, moose, caribou, wolves, mountain climbing Dall Sheep, mountain goats, porcupines, beavers, squirrels, foxes, and 450 different kinds of birds!

21   Weather   Alaska is a windy state. Chinooks are warm winds that melt snow in the middle of winter. Williwaws are sudden, cold winds that can blow up to 115 miles per hour.

22   Geography   Alaska has an interesting landscape. In addition to the mountains, visitors can see tundra which is bare land without trees. There are more than 1,800 islands in Alaska, more than 3 million lakes, and 3,000 rivers.

22   Industry   Alaska ties with Texas as the highest oil-producing state.

24   Geography   What do you know about your own state?

26   Animals   Have you ever seen an Alaskan Husky? Does it remind you of another type of animal? [wolf] Dogs are a domesticated carnivorous mammal. What does that mean?

26   Language   The word "dog" has been used in many slang words and expressions. See if you can guess the meaning:

-You lucky dog [lucky person]!
-That movie was a real dog [uninteresting, bad].
-My dogs are tired from walking [feet].

9

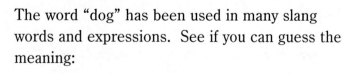

-I feel dog tired [completely].
-They really put on the dog at that party [big display of elegance].

| 27 | Manners | Why is it good to greet people? When is it a good time not to greet people? [When meeting strangers without a guardian] |

30	Math	How many miles longer is the 1,049-mile adult race than the 160-mile kid race?
31	Logic	Why are the dogs missing? What do you think is making them disappear?
33	Animals	Do you have a pet? Do you help take care of it? How? Does your family divide up the responsibilities, or do you do it all?
34	Health	Human athletes also practice and eat extra protein before a race, game, or event.
34	Science	Notice how the dogs adapted to their environment and way of life. How do they eat their fish and drink their water?
42	Vocabulary	A malamute is a powerful breed of dog used as a sled dog. It has thick fur that is white, gray or black. This breed of dogs developed in Alaska.

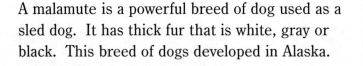

42	Animals	What happens when you feed a homeless or stray dog or cat? [they stick around or come back]
44	Life	Why is teamwork important? Why do they need so many dogs?
45	Math	Each dog can pull two hundred pounds. How many pounds can 16 dogs pull altogether?

10

Alaska State Trivia

The name "Alaska" came from the Aleut word "Alyeska," meaning "The great land." Alyeska was one of Alaska's original names.

Canada is the only country that borders Alaska. The Arctic Ocean, Pacific Ocean, Bering Sea, and Gulf of Alaska are the four bodies of water that border Alaska.

Juneau, the capital of Alaska, is the only U.S. city that is not accessible by road, because of too many glaciers. You have to take a boat or airplane to get there! Alaska has more than 100,000 glaciers!

Alaska is 1,420 miles (2,285 kilometers) from north to south and 2,400 miles (3,862 kilometers) from east to west. Its total area is approximately 615,230 square miles (1,593,323 square kilometers). Its total land area is approximately 570,374 square miles (1,477,155 square kilometers).

(continued)

45	History	Stagecoaches were used before automobiles. Horses pulled these four-wheeled vehicles. The driver had to keep a firm grip on the reins, or the horses would run out of control.
51	Vocabulary	Sleight of hand is used for tricks by magicians and jugglers. Their hands move so quickly that the movements cannot be observed.
53	Food	Maple syrup comes from the sap of the sugar maple tree.
53	Life	Why did Christina and Grant feel like experienced mushers? What do you feel confident doing? Why do you feel this way?

55	Food	Sour, fermented dough is used as leaven to make bread rise. Yeast, a unicellular fungi, is used as leaven in sandwich bread. Bread smells really good while it is baking!
57	Safety	Antifreeze is deadly to people and animals.
57	Vocabulary	Sabotage is the destruction of property or actions by an enemy to hinder or defeat another person.
57	Vocabulary	Veterinarians are doctors who treat all kinds of animal patients. Would you like to be a vet?
58	Feelings	Grant is very worried about Bo. Would you feel embarrassed about crying in front of people? Why or why not?
61	Logic	What are some possible reasons for sending the kids inside instead of letting them watch the vet help the dogs?

11

Alaska State Trivia
(continued)

About one-third of Alaska lies within the Arctic Circle.

Trees cannot grow on the Arctic Coastal Plan in Alaska. It is permafrost or ground that has been frozen for two or more years. In some areas, the ground thaws just enough for wildflowers, mosses, and short grasses to grow. These areas are called tundra.

The unofficial "state bird" of Alaska is the mosquito. These pesky creatures grow really BIG in Alaska!

Alaska is closer to Asia than the lower 48 United States.

Alaska is divided into 16 organized boroughs, which are similar to counties.

Alaska is called "The Land of the Midnight Sun." That is because in the summer, the sun shines 24 hours a day- even at midnight! It is also called the Last Frontier because there is so much of Alaska that is sparsely settled.

Alaska has 39 mountain ranges.

(continued)

65	Life	When are you so excited that you wake up early before sunrise, like Raven and Hunter did?
65	Vocabulary	King behaved like a good leader. What do you think makes a good leader?
66	Vocabulary	Harried means annoyed or disturbed.
66	Vehicles	Although SUVs are popular for their style and space, four-wheel-drive vehicles are a must on the rough and icy terrain common to Alaska.
69	Logic	Why do you think Raven said it was "weird" for Mr. Ryan to race with another friend? How do you feel when your friends do things with other people and don't include you?
71	Hobbies	Do you collect anything? Some collections like stamps, coins, or even trading cards are worth a lot of money.
71	Vocabulary	Beeline means a straight and direct course. Bees go straight back to the beehive after they find pollen.
73	Life	Do you ever check and double check? When?
73	Vocabulary	A pachyderm is a large, hoofed mammal with thick skin like a rhinoceros, hippopotamus or elephant.
75	Logic	What do you think about Mr. Ryan racing his own dogs?
76	Life	What would you do if you won $50,000?

Alaska State Trivia

(continued)

Alaska is the largest of all 50 United States! It is bigger than the three next largest states combined! Alaska's coastline is twice as long as the length of the lower 48 states' coastlines combined! However, Alaska has the lowest population density in the nation.

Iliamna is Alaska's largest lake. It ripples and roars for more than 1,000 square miles (2,590 square kilometers).

Only about 30 percent of the roads in Alaska's highway system are paved!

The largest national forest in the United States is Tongass National Forest in Alaska.

The state of Rhode Island could fit 425 times in the state of Alaska!

Highest recorded temperature: 100° Fahrenheit, Fort Yukon, summer, 1915. Lowest recorded temperature: 80° below zero Fahrenheit, Prospect Creek Camp, winter, 1971.

12

77	Logic	Why can't Raven try to win this year? Why must she wait another year?
77	Culture	Kids and adults like to play blanket toss. This game began long ago when Eskimos would spot faraway animals to hunt by tossing a hunter high into the air on a blanket made of walrus skin. Today, several people could still get into a circle and toss a person on the blanket 20 feet into the air. This activity is similar to bouncing on a trampoline.
77	Writing	Adjectives describe a person, place, or thing. The details of the story make us feel like we are really there. Be sure to use details in your writing.
79	Vocabulary	Hullabaloo means great excitement, noise or uproar. When was the last time you heard a hullabaloo?
84	Logic	What do you think is on Christina's mind? Why does she feel goosebumps?
85	Vocabulary	Grueling means demanding and exhausting.
85	Food	Eskimo ice cream is a popular food in Alaska. It is made from seal oil, snow, and whipped berries. Vegetables in Alaska grow quite large. Cabbages sometimes weigh 95 pounds and carrots can grow to be the size of baseball bats!
86	Language	Boxer Evander Holyfield is called Real Deal Holyfield. What does the expression "the real deal" mean?

13

The Widow's Lamp

In the past, when dog sleds carried people, supplies and mail through Alaska, the safety of the dog sled driver between villages was very important. The drivers relied on roadhouses along the trail for rest and protection.

Whenever a team and driver were on the trail, word was sent to the next roadhouse to let them know. Then the people at the roadhouse would hang a kerosene lamp outside. This helped guide the sled driver to his destination, but also let people know that a team was somewhere out on the trail. The lamp would burn until the driver had reached the roadhouse safely.

The Iditarod carries on this tradition. At the beginning of the race, a lamp, called "the widow's lamp" is hung at the finish line, and burns until the last team has safely crossed that line. It is to let people know there is still a team on the trail, and to watch for them.

Many people think that a race is over when the winner crosses the finish line. But in Alaska, as long as there is a musher and a team of dogs on the trail, people will wait for them at the finish line until they are safely at their destination.

Page-by-page Guide

88 Life — Have you ever been camping? What did you eat? Do you like sardines and beans?

91 Logic — Why do you think the race has a mandatory 24 hour stop? Do you think people would stop if it were not required?

92 Life — What would you miss most if you were competing in the Iditarod race? What would you enjoy about being in the race?

97 History — The Wild West was called wild because of the lawlessness that existed as people moved westward and established new towns.

99 Culture — The first Alaskans were Native Americans who hunted deer and fished for salmon. They created totem poles to represent their family's history. Totem poles tell a story.

102 Vocabulary — Hypothermia is a condition of abnormally low body temperature.

105 Logic — What are all the clues of Sabotage since they began the race?

108 Manners — Why did Grant's parents teach him to speak politely to adults? What do you think of Mr. Ryan's manners?

110 Vocabulary — Renegade means traitor.

110 Logic — Why do you think Mr. Ryan is acting this way?

112 Life — Do you think the kids should have waited for an adult? Why or why not?

Huskies and Malamutes

Huskies and Malamutes are related, and they both love to pull sleds over the icy glaciers of Alaska. But they are two different breeds of dog. Here are some ways to tell them apart:

Alaskan Malamutes are larger than Siberian Huskies. They weigh between 74 and 85 pounds. They are playful, friendly dogs, and very loyal. Malamutes have been know to work so hard for their masters that they died from exhaustion. Malamute coats are black and white or gray and white, and their eyes are brown.

Siberian Huskies come from Siberia, where the breed has been kept pure for hundreds of years. Huskies weigh between 35 and 60 pounds. Their furry coats are gray, tan, or black and white. Their eyes can be green, blue, or brown. This breed is known for its intelligence and gentleness–and, of course, strength!

14

| 117 | Science | The Northern lights, also called the Aurora borealis, is a natural light show that occurs in Alaska's night sky. These sheets of colored light are caused by activity on the sun. |

| 118 | Weather | Black ice is dangerous. It is ice you cannot see until you are right on top of it. This also happens on some city streets during the winter. It is not really the color black, just difficult to see. |

| 118 | Vocabulary | An imposter is a person who deceives by using a fake identity. |

| 118 | Life | Do you think adults ever look down on you and what you think because you are "just a kid?" What can you do about it? |

| 118 | History | Kid power! A thirteen-year-old named Benny Benson entered a contest to design Alaska's state flag and won! His design became Alaska's state flag. A twelve-year-old named Taras Genet became the youngest person to climb Mt. McKinley in 1991. |

| 121 | Logic | What else could Mr. Ryan have done to help his sick sister? |

Be sure to read
Carole Marsh Mystery #9:
The Mystery at Kill Devil Hills

15

Balto

In 1925, a deadly disease called diphtheria threatened the lives of the people who had settled in Nome, Alaska. The people were terribly worried, since they had little time to save themselves and their children. To make matters worse, it was the middle of winter.

There was only one medicine that could cure the disease. The only place in Alaska where the medicine could be found was a hospital in Anchorage, almost 1,000 miles away. The only way to get the medicine all the way from Anchorage was by dog sled.

The people arranged a dog sled relay race to bring a small precious package of medicine across the state to save the town. A team of dogs and a musher waited at each of the 16 designated stations between Anchorage and Nome. When a panting team arrived at a station with the package, there would be a fresh team, waiting to deliver it to the next station.

Speed was extremely important, but the weather was harsh that winter. Temperatures rarely rose above 40° below Fahrenheit. All the drivers and dogs on that race were heroes. One musher hitched himself to his sled when two of his dogs froze to death. News media brought stories of the race as the whole world watched the dramatic race between the dog sleds and time.

(continued)

Discussion Questions

❖ Has a friend ever let you down or betrayed you? What happened? Are you still friends now?

❖ If you had your own plane, what color would it be? What would you name your plane? Where would you fly?

❖ Christina and Grant ate buffalo, caribou and many other Alaskan foods they would not normally eat. Have you ever been so hungry that you ate something you would not ordinarily try? What was it?

❖ If you could visit Alaska, what would you like to see? Which activities would you try? Which new foods would you taste?

❖ Do you think Mr. Rutledge and Mr. Ryan will still be friends? Why or why not?

❖ Did you learn anything new about Alaska? What did you learn?

❖ Imagine that you are on a dogsled in the Iditarod race. Describe how you are feeling and what you see.   Tell us about your spirit of competition and your great skill in driving your team of dogs. Use lots of adjectives!

16

Balto
(continued)

On the second last section of the relay, Gunnar Kaasen and his lead sled dog Balto waited anxiously in Bluff, Alaska for the medicine to arrive so they could bring it the rest of the way to Nome. The second it arrived, the team dashed off to Nome as fast as they could.

Gunnar and Balto endured one of the roughest parts of the entire journey. His dogs got stuck in snowdrifts, the sled was overturned and the medicine was almost lost, the team almost fell through a crack in the ice, and a blizzard blinded Gunnar.

But Balto, the lead sled dog, remained calm. He patiently led his team around the dangers and bravely guided them, even in the blinding blizzard. Without stopping for 20 consecutive hours, the dog team pulled the sled for 53 miles until they arrived, too tired to even bark, in Nome.

The people of Nome were saved from the deadly diphtheria! Balto became an international hero overnight as stories of his courage and bravery spread across the globe. Since that great and brave adventure of 1925, Alaska has re-created that dramatic race across the state every year. The Iditarod.

Hero

1. Draw a map of Alaska. Label major landmarks, streets, roads, bridges, waterways, monuments, and bodies of water. Include a key, map symbols, title, and chart of locations.

2. Juneau is the only U.S. capital that is not accessible by road because of the glaciers. Visitors must travel by plane or boat. Design some unique modes of transportation to reach Juneau, the capital city of Alaska.

3. Compare the small suburb of Peachtree City (where Grant and Christina live) with any of the small towns the mushers encounter in Alaska. What are some differences between the two places? What are some similarities? List some benefits to living in each location.

4. How is Juneau unique in comparison to major U.S. cities in the continental states like Chicago, Los Angles, New York, Miami, and Washington, D.C.?

5. Construct a toothpick model of a major bridge or railroad in Alaska. Add various landmarks and surrounding cities.

6. Design a new trail for the Iditarod Trail Sled Dog Race in Alaska. Use your imagination. You could cross the Bering Strait, go into Canada, cross mountains, whatever you think would be challenging. Draw your new race course on a poster.

7. Alaska is surrounded by four bodies of water: the Arctic Ocean, Bering Sea, Pacific Ocean, and the Gulf of Alaska. Use blue yarn to create these bodies of water around your Alaska map project. Use green yarn to mark where Canada meets Alaska on the state's eastern border.

17

Northern Lights

Alaska is famous for many things, but one special state feature is the spectacular nighttime light show called the Aurora Borealis, or the Northern lights. As night falls, in the spring or autumn, the sky is lit up with what looks like shimmering, flowing curtains of colored light, draping purples, blues, reds, and greens, far up into the starry sky.

The Northern lights are caused by a natural process that takes place in the earth's atmosphere. The sun releases atomic particles, like electrons and protons into space. Some of these billions of particles drift towards the earth.

The earth has a magnetic pull around it because of the iron core at the center of the earth. This magnetic force pulls the particles to the most northern and southern parts of the globe. As the particles hit the earth's atmosphere they interact with the gases that make up the atmosphere. This interaction produces the beautiful currents of color.

Mathematics: Calculate It!

1. A group of 10 hungry mushers want to order an Eskimo Pie in Alaska. Each person wants to eat 4 slices of pie. If the pies are each cut in 8 slices, how many pies must the group order?

2. Goldrusher Gwen looks for gold in Alaska 8 hours each day. She doesn't like to work on Sunday, because that's when she hunts for berries and goes fishing. At the end of the first week, Gwen finds 14 golden nuggets. She discovers 37 golden nuggets the second week. During the third week, Gwen unearths 42 golden nuggets. At the end of her last week in Alaska, Gwen uncovers 75 golden nuggets. How many hours has Gwen spent searching for gold? How many golden nuggets did she find?

3. A ferry company operates 6 ferries. If each ferry can carry 275 passengers, how many passengers can the ferries carry all together?

4. A budget is a list of expenses. Total this budget for the Alaska mystery trip: $2,200–airfare, $450–meals, $600-lodging, $175–rental car, $300-parkas and winter gear, $50–souvenirs.

5. There are 50 mushers competing in the Junior Iditarod race. Each musher has a team of 16 dogs. If each dog needs two sets of booties to keep warm, how many booties will each musher need? How many booties will the competitors need (total)?

6. The Northern Lights are caused by electrons and protons that shoot out from the sun. These charged particles drift around in space and are pulled into the Earth's magnetic field. They strike gas particles in the atmosphere and turn on the northern lights! Lights showers can occur as low as 40 miles above the Earth's surface and extend for hundreds of miles into space! How many feet equal 40 miles? (Hint: There are 5,280 feet in one mile).

Gold Rush

"North to Alaska!"

That is where as many as 100,000 men and some women and children rushed, after gold was found in Sitka in 1872. In 1880, Joe Juneau and Dick Harris struck gold near the place that would later be named after Juneau and become the capital of the state. Rumors of gold "strikes," or gold finds, spread like wildfire across America. Men flocked to Alaska in droves, setting up "tent cities" and panning for gold.

For more than 30 years, gold deposits were found in many sites across Alaska and the Yukon. In 1907, the largest gold nugget ever found in Alaska was unearthed near Nome. It weighed 107 ounces, and measured 7 inches long and 4 inches wide.

The gold rush is an important part of Alaskan history. The event attracted many settlers to the state. With people came roads and buildings, so trade and transportation flourished, which spurred the development of towns and cities where wilderness had been.

English: Write It!

1. Write an ode to the heroic dog Balto that is either silly or serious. Include historical facts about his journey and life.

2. Which character did you like best in the mystery book? Why? What would you change about that person if you could? In what ways would you like to be more like that person?

3. Pretend you are a Siberian husky or malamute dog that runs with a sled dog team around Alaska. How do you feel about your job? Do you like the other dogs and your master? What do you like best to eat? Write a story about some adventures this sled dog might have out on the trail.

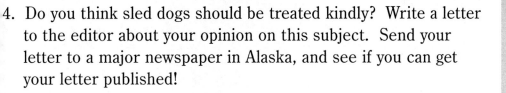

4. Do you think sled dogs should be treated kindly? Write a letter to the editor about your opinion on this subject. Send your letter to a major newspaper in Alaska, and see if you can get your letter published!

5. Write three diary entries from the perspective of an Alaska native who has just crossed the Bering Strait from Asia to live in North America. What are your first few days in Alaska like? Are you glad you came or do you want to go home? What chores do you have? How does your family survive?

6. Write a biography of a famous musher like Susan Butcher or Joe Redington Sr. Include their most important victories and accomplishments.

7. Write a new ending for the last chapter of the mystery.

Children's Books

- Anderson, LaVere. *Balto--Sled Dog of Alaska.* Illustrated by Herman B. Vestal. Grades 3-5.

- Bacon, Ethel. *To See the Moon.* Illustrated by David Ray. Grades 2-4.

- Blake, Robert J. *Akiak: A Tale from the Iditarod.* Illustrated by the author. Grades 2-4.

- Cooper, Michael. *Racing Sled Dogs: An Original North American Sport.* Grades 2-6.

- Crisman, Ruth. *Racing the Iditarod Trail.* Grades 4-8.

- Devine, Monica. *The Iditarod: The Greatest Win Ever.* Grades 3-6.

- Dolan, Ellen M. *Susan Butcher and the Iditarod Trail.* Grades 4-8.

- Gardiner, John Reynolds. *Stone Fox.* Illustrated by Marcia Sewell. Grades 2-5.

- Gill, Shelley. *Kiana's Iditarod.* Illustrations by Shannon Cartwright. Grades 1-3.

- Gill, Shelley and Libby Riddles. *Danger the Dog Yard Cat.* Illustrated by Shannon Cartwright. Grades K-4.

- Harter, Lois. *Where's the Boss - A Sleddog's tale from Alaska's Iditarod Trail.* Illustrated by Dave Totten. Grades 3 to 6.

- Jackson, Joan. *Elim--The Determined Athlete.* Illustrated by Robert S. Gilmore. Grades 2-5.

- Kramer, S.A. *Adventure in Alaska.* Grades 2-5.

- London, Jack. *The Call of the Wild.* Grades 4 and up.

- London, Jack. *White Fang.* Illustrated by Philippe Munch. Grades 4 and up.

(continued)

Vocabulary: Spell It!

Study the words below. All of them are taken from the mystery book. Fold the page in half and take a spelling test! Check your work, and study the words you miss! Look up each word in the dictionary and write its definition on a separate piece of paper.

PRICELESS _____

OFFICIAL _____

GLIMMERING _____

GRATITUDE _____

PASTEL _____

DETOUR _____

CEREMONIAL _____

ARCTIC _____

CACHET _____

FUMBLE _____

PACHYDERM _____

HARNESS _____

RAVENOUS _____

SPAWN _____

DEVOUR _____

SHARD _____

TERMINOLOGY _____

PERMISSION _____

UNISON _____

MOUSTACHE _____

FUNGUS _____

ANCESTOR _____

POISON _____

VETERINARIAN _____

LISTLESS _____

Children's Books
(continued)

• O'Dell, Scott. *Black Star, Bright Dawn.* Grades 3 and up.

• Paulsen, Gary. *Dogsong.* Grades 5 and up.

• Paulsen, Gary. *Dogteam.* Illustrated by Ruth Wright Paulsen. Grades K-3+.

• Paulsen, Gary. *My Life in Dog Years.* Grades 4 and up.

• Paulsen, Gary. *Puppies, Dogs, and Blue Northers: Reflections on Being Raised by a Pack of Sled Dogs.* Illustrated by Ruth Wright Paulsen. Grades 4 and up.

• Paulsen, Gary. *Woodsong.* Grades 4 and up.

• Riddles, Libby. *Storm Run.* Illustrations by Shannon Cartwright. Grades 4-6.

• Shahan, Sherry. *Dashing Through the Snow: The Story of the Junior Iditarod.* Grades 3-6.

• Shields, Mary. *Happy Dog Trilogy: Can Dogs Talk? Secret Messages--Training a Happy Dog; Loving a Happy Dog.* Grades 2-4.

• Seibert, Patricia. *Mush: Across Alaska in the World's Longest Sled-Dog Race.* Grades K-5.

• Standiford, Natalie. *The Bravest Dog Ever--The True Story of Balto.* Illustrated by Donald Cook. Grades 1-3.

• Ungermann, Kenneth A. *The Race to Nome.* Grades 2 and up.

• Wadsworth, Ginger. *Susan Butcher: Sled Dog Racer.* Grades 3-6.

• Wood, Ted. *Iditarod Dreams: Dusty and His Sled Dogs Compete in Alaska's Junior Iditarod.* Grades 2-6.

1. Sketch portraits of each mystery book character. Add specific details in the background like a dog, sled, mountain, snow, etc.

2. Paint a picture of cheering crowds welcoming the mushers at the end of the Iditarod Trail Sled Dog Race in Nome, Alaska!

3. Build an igloo with marshmallows. Freeze your igloo to make it stick together better! Add details like an Inuit family made of mini-marshmallows, a mountain of whipped cream, and a frozen lake with gummy fish.

4. Alaska has 39 mountain ranges. Of the 20 highest peaks in the United States, Alaska can claim 17! Draw a picture of the view from the twin-peaked Mount McKinley, the highest mountain in North America. It was originally called Denali, "The Great One" by Alaskan Natives.

5. Design a new cover for *The Mystery on Alaska's Iditarod Trail* book. You could take photographs or draw your own pictures. Create a new and interesting font!

6. Choose a city in Alaska, big or small. Gather craft materials like fabric, cotton balls, paint, cardboard, toothpicks, buttons, grass, yarn, etc. to build a miniature version of this city. Construct a three-dimensional city using miniature objects. Don't forget to mark major cities, geographical landmarks, and events of historic interest. You could even make an edible version and eat it with your pals!

7. Sculpt a mountain and create a shadow box. Paint a sunset on the inside of the box. Use colorful ribbons of bright red, orange, and purple hues for your Alaskan sunset!

8. Use modeling clay to create a Siberian husky or a malamute dog. Ask an adult to help you "bake" the clay so it will harden. Set the dog in front of your dog sled craft!

Dog Sled Websites

Everything Husky: links for the world of dog-powered or dog-assisted sports
www.everythinghusky.com

Cool Dreams: interactive site for teachers and students with quizzes and forums
www.cooldreams.com

Sled Dogs: sleddog racing and huskies online resource
www.sleddog.com

Race Dogs: Scandinavian and European mushing
www.racedogs.com

Manitoba Dog Sledding Association: articles, local trail maps, and links
www.autobahn.mb.ca/~mdsa/home.html

Happy Huskies Sled Dog Site: breeds, photos, Alaskan Husky facts, quiz, list of sled dog names
www.angelfire.com/on3/happy huskies/

Our Alaskan Cyber-Cabin: site hosted by family who raises, works with, and runs a team of Alaskan huskies in Alaska
www.alaska.net/~dogdrivr

Sled Dog Central: Sled dog news, interviews, kennel tips
www.sleddogcentral.com

Mushing & Dog Sled Racing: dog sledding, skijoring, the Iditarod race, links
www.husky-petlove.com/mushing.html

Alaska is known for its excellent food. Try baking this famous dish to share with your friends!

Baked Alaska

Ingredients

Serves 12

1 1/3 cups graham cracker crumbs
1/4 cup white sugar
1/4 cup butter, softened
4 cups vanilla ice cream
3 egg whites
1/4 teaspoon salt
1 teaspoon almond extract
6 tablespoons white sugar

Directions

1. Preheat oven to 375°F.
2. Set aside 3 tablespoons of the graham cracker crumbs for a topping.
3. Mix remaining crumbs, sugar, and softened butter together. Press the mixture into a 9-inch pie plate.
4. Bake the crust at 375°F for 10 minutes. Cool the crust, and then chill it in the freezer.
5. Pack firm vanilla ice cream into the chilled crust. Place the dish back in the freezer.
6. Beat egg whites until they are frothy. Add salt and almond extract. Gradually add sugar. Beat mixture until it looks stiff and glossy.
7. Spread mixture over the ice cream, sealing off each edge.
8. Sprinkle the remaining graham cracker crumbs over the mixture.
9. Place dish under broiler (500°F) for 2 minutes. Serve immediately!

 NOTE: The preparation of all dishes are to be carried out with the supervision of an adult.

Candy Cane Hot Chocolate

Ingredients

4 cups milk
1 cup whipped cream
4 crushed candy canes
4 mini candy canes
3 squares (1 ounce) semi sweet chocolate, chopped

Directions

In a saucepan, heat milk until steaming, but not boiling. Add the chocolate and crushed candies. Whisk until smooth and melted. Pour into mugs, top with whipped cream and add a mini cane stir stick!

Snow Punch

Ingredients

1 can fruit punch
2 pints vanilla ice cream, softened
2 cups Sprite, chilled

Directions

Combine fruit punch, vanilla ice cream, and Sprite in a punch bowl. Stir until blended. Chill and serve.

Cranberry Apple Cider

Ingredients

1 quart cranberry juice
1 quart apple juice
2 oranges, zested
14 whole cloves
1 1/2 cups dried cranberries
1 tsp. vanilla extract
1 1/3 cups honey
2 cinnamon sticks

Directions

Pour cranberry and apple juice into a large saucepan and cook over medium heat. Add the orange zest, cloves, cranberries, vanilla extract, honey, and cinnamon sticks. Heat until hot and steamy (about 20 minutes) and stir occasionally.

The Mystery on Alaska's Iditarod Trail Maze

Help Christina, Grant, Raven, and Hunter race through the Iditarod Trail in Alaska!

23

The Mystery on Alaska's Iditarod Trail
Pair Up

Match the words on the left with the correct words on the right!

IDITAROD	SLED
NORTHERN	BUCKLE
CHECK	ALASKA
BELT	RUSH
UNITED STATES	TRAIL
JUNIOR	DOUGH
ANCHORAGE	POINTS
DOG	IDITAROD
GOLD	LIGHTS
SOUR	POSTAL SERVICE

24

The Mystery on the Iditarod Trail Dog Sled Craft

Make your own dog sled!

Materials: several clean popsicle sticks, flat wooden toothpicks, wood glue, wire cutters, one long white pipecleaner

Lay two popsicle sticks down for runners. Cut two sticks in half. Lay two halves on each other and glue them on the runners, one on each end. Leave a small amount of space on each end. Let it dry

Lay four sticks down in the exact middle of the runners (next to one another) as a flat base. Glue them down so that one end fits squarely and the other end sticks out over the runners. Allow it to dry.

Cut four more sticks in half. Glue five of the halves together as shown laying the pieces on two more stick halves, which will serve as the back support. Glue one half at the very bottom of the piece and one at the top, but leave a little room at the top so the five curved tops still show (see picture).

Glue the piece from Step #3 on the end of the runners where the base ends squarely.

Glue two sticks as rails along the base. The flat part of the sticks should face sideways. Glue the tops next to the vertical piece and the bottoms next to the base. The rails should slope downward like a slide.

Cut flat toothpicks in three different heights. Make two equal sets of cut toothpicks. Glue them to the side rails and runners at the intervals shown.

Cut two small sections of pipecleaner and arch them.

Glue one arch at the end of the base for the front of the basket. Glue the other at the top for a handlebar as shown.

Note: Ask an adult to help you with the wirecutters or pliers!

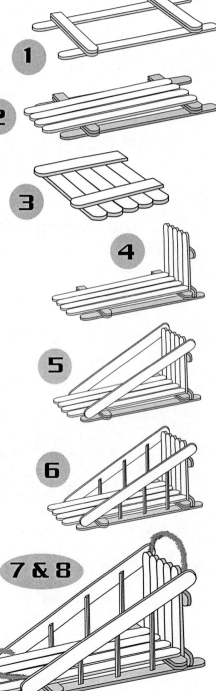

25

The Mystery on Alaska's Iditarod Trail Sourdough Expedition Rebus!

In the winter of 1909, seven miners or "sourdoughs" led by Tom Lloyd decided to climb Nort. America's highest peak–Mount McKinley. Seven set out; none had any climbing experience. Three turned back. Billy Taylor, Pete Anderson, and Charley McGonagall joined Tom Lloyd in the ascen.

Use the rebus clues to complete the statements.

1. This is what a "Sourdough" is. The term "Sourdough" referred to a miner or

    an  + [clock] + er = __ __ __ - __ __ __ __ __, the opposite of a gr + [leg] +

    n + [bread] = __ __ __ __ __ __ __ __ __.

2. The name "Sourdough" came from the yeasty [star] + ter =

    __ __ __ __ __ __ __ used to make br + [head] -h + s = __ __ __ __ __ __ which we

    [stapler] - r = __ __ __ __ __ __ part of the miners' diets.

3. The miners climbed, without ropes, while carrying a [flag] + [fishing pole] =

    __ __ __ __ __ __ __ __ to plant at the summit. For 18 hours, the sourdoughs

    climbed up and up.

4. Remarkably, two men made it all the way to the top. Unfortunately, it was the

    north peak; the s + [mouth/teeth] - m + p + [turkey] - b =

    __ __ __ __ __ __   __ __ __ __ is actually higher.

5. The Sourdough X + [bed] + e + [leg] = __ __ __ __ __ __ __ __ __ __ __

    is still considered one of mountain climbing's most amazing [feet] + s - e + a =

    __ __ __ __ __.

26

The Mystery on Alaska's Iditarod Trail Word Search

Search for the mysteriously hidden words below!

```
G  R  E  H  S  U  M  A  E  U  N  T  B  P  E  Z  I
L  A  P  R  G  O  L  D  R  U  S  H  S  K  X  D  S
R  C  M  B  W  L  D  G  M  A  B  S  A  E  I  E  B
B  E  L  T  B  U  C  K  L  E  W  C  O  T  P  L  R
E  K  K  A  T  G  S  A  M  F  N  O  A  E  G  S  A
W  R  C  O  U  R  S  E  R  A  J  R  M  P  O  T  K
I  S  U  F  A  K  A  R  P  S  O  N  M  M  G  U  E
N  L  C  Y  A  C  T  I  B  D  D  S  N  O  W  A  C
D  V  E  S  O  O  M  D  L  O  G  D  D  C  W  E  S
```

ALASKA	DOG	IDITAROD	GOLD RUSH
SLED	COMPETE	PANCAKE	WIND
RACE	COURSE	SNOW	MOOSE
MUSHER	TRAIL	BELT BUCKLE	BRAKE

27

The Mystery on Alaska's Iditarod Trail
Fill-in-the-Blank Crossword

Fill in the blanks to find the missing attractions in our nation's capital!

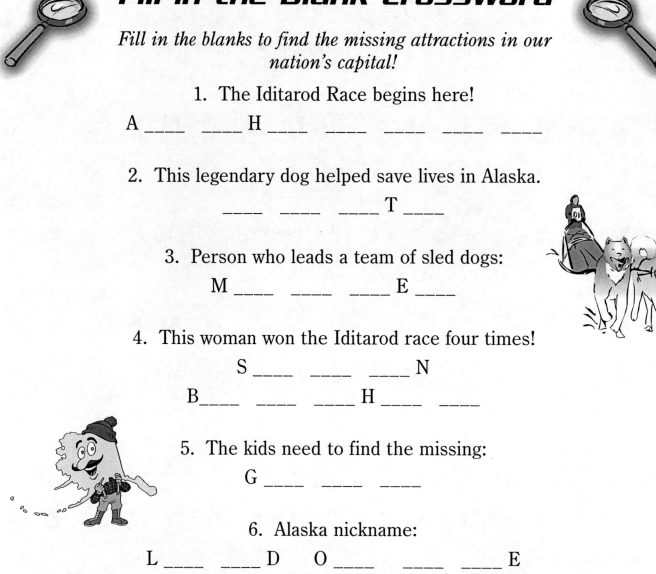

1. The Iditarod Race begins here!

A ____ ____ H ____ ____ ____ ____ ____

2. This legendary dog helped save lives in Alaska.

____ ____ ____ T ____

3. Person who leads a team of sled dogs:

M ____ ____ ____ E ____

4. This woman won the Iditarod race four times!

S ____ ____ ____ N

B____ ____ ____ H ____ ____

5. The kids need to find the missing:

G ____ ____ ____

6. Alaska nickname:

L ____ ____ D   O ____ ____ ____ E

____ ____ ____ N ____ ____ ____ T   S ____ ____

7. Musher and historian who organized the first Iditarod Trail Sled Dog Race:

J____ ____   R____ ____ ____ N ____ ____ ____ ____ SR.

&

D____ ____ ____ ____ ____ Y ____ ____ ____ E

28

Activities

The Mystery on Alaska's Iditarod Trail
Matching Characters

Match these mystery characters with their descriptions!

1. Raven   A. sneaky magician

2. Mr. Rutledge   B. knowledgeable about dogs

3. Christina   C. loves Bo the dog

4. Mimi   D. owns a dog sled training camp

5. Grant   E. pilot who play golf

6. Hunter   F. mystery writer

7. Papa   G. anticipates riding in the Junior Iditarod

8. Mr. Ryan   H. mystery-solving sister

29

The Mystery on Alaska's Iditarod Trail Quiz

Use the clues to answer the questions!

1. Alaska became the 50th state in the year:

   _____

2. Valuable missing objects in the mystery:

   _____

3. Alaska is the largest American:

   _____

4. Disease that inspired the first Iditarod run in 1925:

   _____

5. Mr. Ryan said he committed his crimes to raise money to:

   _____

6. According to official Iditarod rules, each team may harness:

   _____

7. The United States bought Alaska from Russia for:

   _____

8. Musher teams carry a ceremonial:

   _____

9. On the Iditarod Trail, the children's sled almost ran into a big:

   _____

30

The Mystery on Alaska's Iditarod Trail
True or False

Mark each statement true or false.
Can you replace the word (or words) that is false in each statement?

_____ 1. Mr. Ryan was a dog trainer and a magician.

_____ 2. Alaska's Mount McKinley is the highest mountain in South America.

_____ 3. There are many different kinds of cultures in Alaska.

_____ 4. The winner of the Iditarod Trail Sled Dog Race receives $30,000.

_____ 5. Thousands of prospectors came to Alaska during the Gold Rush.

_____ 6. In 1925, mushers drove dog sleds from Anchorage to Nome to bring an antidotal serum to cure a virus called diphtheria.

_____ 7. The kids are looking for the missing silver bars and their sled cats.

_____ 8. The lead dog of Mr. Rutledge's team was named Queen.

_____ 9. Juneau is the capital city of Alaska.

_____ 10. The original inhabitants of Alaska were the Inuit, Aleut, and Indian groups.

31

Math Activities
1. 5 pies; 2. 192 hours, 168 nuggets; 3. 1,650 passengers; 4. $3,775 budget; 5. 128 booties per musher, 6,400 booties total; 6. 211,200 feet

The Mystery on Alaska's Iditarod Trail Pair Up
IDITAROD TRAIL; NORTHERN LIGHTS; CHECK POINTS; BELTBUCKLE; UNITED STATES POSTAL SERVICE; JUNIOR IDITAROD; ANCHORAGE, ALASKA; DOG SLED; GOLD RUSH; SOUR DOUGH

The Mystery on Alaska's Iditarod Trail Sourdough Expedition Rebus!
1-OLD-TIMER, GREENHORN; 2-STARTER, BREADS, STAPLE; 3-FLAGPOLE;
4-SOUTH PEAK; 5-EXPEDITION, FEATS

The Mystery on Alaska's Iditarod Trail Fill-in-the-Blank Crossword
1. Anchorage; 2. Balto; 3. musher; 4. Susan Butcher; 5. gold; 6. Land of the Midnight Sun;
7. Joe Redington Sr. & Dorothy Page

The Mystery on Alaska's Iditarod Trail Matching Characters
1-G; 2-D; 3-H; 4-F; 5-C; 6-B; 7-E; 8-A

The Mystery on Alaska's Iditarod Trail Quiz
1. 1959; 2. golden bars; 3. state; 4. diphtheria; 5. help his sister with cancer treatment bills
6. 16 dogs; 7. two cents an acre; 8. cachet of mail; 9. moose

The Mystery on Alaska's Iditarod Trail True or False?
1-T; 2-F (North America); 3-T; 4-F ($50,000); 5-T; 6-T; 7-F (golden bars and sled dogs);
8-F (King); 9-T; 10-T

32